# Hillary Rodham Clinton

## by Jill C. Wheeler

Breaking Barriers

# visit us at
# www.abdopub.com

Published by ABDO & Daughters, an imprint of ABDO Publishing Company, 4940 Viking Drive, Suite 622, Edina, Minnesota 55435. Copyright ©2003 by Abdo Consulting Group, Inc. International copyrights reserved in all countries. No part of this book may be reproduced in any form without written permission from the publisher.

Printed in the United States.

Edited by Paul Joseph
Graphic Design: John Hamilton
Cover Design: Mighty Media
Interior Photos: AP/Photo, p. 1, 5, 6, 9, 13, 14, 17, 19, 21, 22, 25, 26, 29, 31, 33, 35, 36, 39, 41, 44, 47, 49, 50, 53, 55, 57, 59, 60, 61
Digital Stock, p. 10
John Hamilton, p. 43

### Library of Congress Cataloging-in-Publication Data

Wheeler, Jill C., 1964-
    Hillary Rodham Clinton / Jill C. Wheeler.
        p. cm. — (Breaking barriers)
    Summary: A biography of former First Lady Hillary Clinton, from her "perfect" childhood and college years through her political life in Arkansas and Washington, D.C. to her election as senator from New York.
        ISBN 1-57765-741-1
        1. Clinton, Hillary Rodham—Juvenile literature. 2. Presidents' spouses—United States—Biography—Juvenile literature. 3. Legislators—United States—Biography—Juvenile literature. 4. United States. Congress. Senate—Biography—Juvenile literature. [1. Clinton, Hillary Rodham. 2. First ladies. 3. Legislators. 4. Women—Biography.] I. Title.

E887.C55 W48 2002
973.931'092—dc21
[B]
                                                    2002018768

# Contents

# A Lady of Firsts

*I*t was a warm spring day in May 1992 at the all-female school, Wellesley College. It was graduation day and the students were buzzing about their commencement speaker. The speaker was a Wellesley alumna. She was also the wife of a candidate running for president of the United States.

In her address, the speaker reminded the graduates that they had many more career choices than their mothers had at their age. "You may choose to be a corporate executive or a rocket scientist," she told them. "You may run for public office, you may choose to stay home and raise your children. But you can now make any or all of those choices and they can be the work of your life."

The ideas were not new to the Wellesley graduates. But for the speaker, Hillary Rodham Clinton, they were a critical part of her life.

When Hillary graduated from Wellesley in 1969, the college was known for producing "good wives." At that time, few people expected women to have careers. Most women thought they had little choice in what to do with their lives. Hillary spent her life working so women would have more choices than simply being "good wives."

*Hillary Rodham Clinton*

*Hillary Rodham Clinton with her husband, President Bill Clinton.*

In the course of her life, the woman who became first lady of the United States blazed many trails. She was the first Wellesley student asked to speak at her own commencement ceremony. She was the first first lady to be assigned an important political position in the government. And she was the first woman to be elected to the U.S. Senate from New York. Some people even say she might be the first woman to become president.

Her husband, former president Bill Clinton, agrees with that possibility. "I've always liked strong women. It doesn't bother me for people to see her and get excited and say she could be president. I always say she could be president, too."

Throughout her life, Hillary has gone where few women have dared to go. She changed what it means to be the first lady. Her journey has not always been easy. She has made close friends and powerful enemies along the way. However, friends and enemies alike recognize her keen mind and her unique strength in good and bad times.

# Growing Up In Park Ridge

*H*illary Diane Rodham was born on October 26, 1947, in Chicago, Illinois. She and her parents, Hugh and Dorothy Rodham, lived in an apartment until Hillary was three years old. When they had saved enough money, they moved to a yellow brick home in the quiet Chicago suburb of Park Ridge, Illinois.

For Hugh and Dorothy, owning a home in a middle-class suburb was a dream come true. Both had grown up during the Great Depression. Hugh was born into a poor family in Scranton, Pennsylvania. A gifted athlete, he attended college on a football scholarship. He also worked in a coal mine to make extra money for school.

After graduating, Hugh moved to Chicago and worked as a salesman for a company that made curtains. While there, he met a young woman named Dorothy Howell in 1937. She was applying for a job as a secretary. She had moved to Chicago from California. The couple began dating and fell in love.

*Hillary Rodham Clinton*

*Hugh Rodham served in the U.S. Navy during World War II.*

However, across the sea in Europe, World War II was brewing. The war interrupted Hugh and Dorothy's romance when Hugh served in the navy. In 1942, they were finally able to get married, and soon began a family.

Hugh ran his family much like the troops he trained in the navy. He always expected the best of his children, especially first-born Hillary. He was hard on himself as well. After the war, he started his own curtain business. He designed, sewed, and even hung the curtains himself. Dorothy stayed home to raise Hillary and her two younger brothers, Hugh, Jr., and Tony.

Hillary had a happy childhood. Many children lived in her neighborhood, and they all played together. The city had very little crime. Her parents never had to worry about Hillary or her brothers. "They just said, 'Be back in time for dinner,'" Hillary remembered.

When she was four, Hillary learned an important lesson about standing up for herself. A neighborhood girl named Suzy always picked on her. When Hillary came home crying after an encounter with the tough little girl, Dorothy talked to Hillary. "You're going to have to stand up to her," she told Hillary. "The next time she hits you, I want you to hit back." The next time Suzy picked on Hillary, Hillary closed her eyes, punched Suzy, and knocked her down. Suzy never picked on Hillary again.

From the beginning, Hillary was a natural leader. She had a special ability to organize events and motivate people. She also liked to try a little of everything. She took piano and ballet lessons, and she joined the Girl Scouts. While she never enjoyed the piano lessons and eventually quit them, she earned almost every merit badge in Girl Scouts. Hillary also loved baseball, just like her father. They would go to watch the Chicago Cubs play. Hillary quickly memorized the players' statistics. She could quote them as well as any boy in her class.

At Eugene Field Elementary School and Emerson Junior High, Hillary excelled in all her classes. But her father still encouraged her to do better. She usually brought home a report card with all A's. One time her father looked at the card and said, "You must go to a pretty easy school."

Hugh Rodham was a loving but firm father. He made sure his children learned the value of hard work. When it came time to weed the lawn, he paid Hillary and her brothers a penny for each dandelion they pulled.

The family never had an abundance of nice things. Hugh believed there was no need to buy new clothes unless the old clothes were completely worn out. At night, he sometimes turned off the heat even though the children complained about the cold. The Rodham family was also among the last in Park Ridge to get a television.

Hugh taught his children how to survive in the real world. Meanwhile, Dorothy also taught her daughter how to thrive in a world that men dominated. She raised Hillary to believe that girls were just as good as boys. She told her there was nothing she couldn't do or say just because she was a girl.

*Hillary Rodham Clinton holds her cat, Socks.*

*Hillary Rodham Clinton talks to four-year-old Brea Spence during a stop at the Next Door Foundation, on September 17, 1996, in Milwaukee, Wisconsin.*

Hillary was surprised to learn that not everyone believed boys and girls had the same abilities. When she was 13, Hillary wrote to the National Aeronautics and Space Administration (NASA). She asked them about training to become an astronaut. NASA wrote back to her and said girls couldn't be astronauts.

Hillary was furious. Later she learned astronauts need excellent eyesight. Hillary had worn thick glasses since she was in grade school. So she accepted that she couldn't become an astronaut, even if they had allowed girls.

# Changing the World

*E*ven when she was young, Hillary's friends noticed that she wanted to make a difference in the world. Hillary knew her life was easy compared to others. Her father, who remembered working in the coal mines, made sure she knew that other people suffered more than she did. He took Hillary and her brothers to visit the coal mines so they would understand the hard work others must endure. Hillary became convinced that she wanted to do what she could to make life better for others.

Hillary found an outlet for her desire to help others at her church. The First United Methodist Church had a special pastor just for young people. His name was the Reverend Don Jones. Reverend Jones had just graduated from the seminary. He loved working with young people. He talked about topics that interested them. And he wanted to show them that not all neighborhoods were like Park Ridge.

*Hillary Rodham Clinton*

Reverend Jones took Hillary and her friends to hear a speech by the Reverend Dr. Martin Luther King, Jr. Jones introduced them to young African-American and Hispanic people who lived in poor Chicago neighborhoods. This was new for many of the Park Ridge kids. In Park Ridge, nearly everyone was white.

Reverend Jones also took the youth group to visit local farms. Many of the farms hired migrant workers to help plant, tend, and harvest the crops. Hillary learned that many of the children of migrant workers were left alone during the day. Few had the opportunity to go to school. This bothered Hillary. She thought it was unfair that she could go to school and the migrants' children could not.

Hillary worked to change the situation. When the church began sending older teens to baby-sit the migrant children, Hillary got involved. She held fundraisers to help pay for the baby-sitting services. Her fundraisers, which included a sports tournament, got everyone involved. "Mothers in the neighborhood were amazed at how they couldn't get their boys to do much," Dorothy Rodham recalled. "But Hillary had them all running around."

In the fall of 1960, Hillary started high school at Maine East High School. Once again, she proved herself a top scholar. She served in student government and was part of the National Honor

*Reverend Dr. Martin Luther King, Jr.*

Society. She also began to see some changes in her friends that concerned her.

"I saw a lot of my friends who had been really lively and smart... beginning to worry that boys would think they were too smart... " she said. "Or beginning to cut back on how well they did or the courses they took, because that's not where their boyfriends were."

Hillary refused to fall into that trap. She didn't wear makeup because she didn't think it was important. She continued to say what was on her mind, even when there were boys nearby.

If anything, Hillary could be too blunt in her statements. She always said exactly what was on her mind, even at the risk of offending other people. Throughout her life, she would continue to stand up for what she believed in. Yet sometimes, people did not agree with her actions.

In November 1963, Hillary and her classmates heard about the assassination of President John F. Kennedy. Kennedy's death shocked and saddened the students. They sensed that the politics of America were changing. In the 1960s, people were beginning to question the way things were. Politics were an important part of that.

Hugh Rodham had always supported Republican candidates. As the 1964 election approached, he supported the Republican candidate running for president, Barry Goldwater. Hillary also supported Goldwater and campaigned for him at her school. By this time, she had transferred to Maine South High School where she was a senior.

*Senator Barry Goldwater with President John F. Kennedy at the White House in September 1963.*

*First Lady Hillary Rodham Clinton in 1995.*

At Maine, one of the teachers staged a mock election. Hillary volunteered to represent Goldwater in the campaign. Another classmate volunteered to represent the Democratic candidate, Lyndon Johnson. Then the teacher made a surprise switch. He told Hillary she had to give a speech urging students to vote for Johnson. The other student had to give a speech urging students to vote for Goldwater. The students voted for Goldwater, as did most residents of Park Ridge. However, Hillary gained valuable public speaking experience.

Hillary ran for president of her class but lost. She also worked on the school newspaper and was involved in many extracurricular activities. She was named Most Likely to Succeed in her class. At her high school graduation ceremony, her name was called for so many honors and awards that her mother was embarrassed.

For spring break of her senior year, Hillary took a trip to Florida with her girlfriends. It was Hillary's first long-distance trip without her family. Her next trip would also take her far from Illinois, to the East Coast and Wellesley College.

# Wellesley

*W*ellesley College, near Boston, Massachusetts, was one of the country's top colleges for women. At that time, Ivy League schools such as Yale, Dartmouth, and Princeton did not accept female students. Hillary chose Wellesley because it was an excellent school. It was also far away from her father's strict rules. She did not visit the campus before she enrolled. She'd only seen pictures, but she liked what she saw.

When Hillary entered Wellesley in 1965, the United States was in the middle of vast political and social changes. The Civil Rights movement was in full swing under the leadership of Martin Luther King, Jr. People were beginning to question the growing conflict in Vietnam. In the coming years, college campuses would become the scene for demonstrations and protests on these and other issues.

For Hillary, starting at Wellesley meant she had to prove herself to others. All of the women who had been accepted into Wellesley were smart. In order to compete with them, Hillary would have to work even harder than she had in high school.

Hillary Rodham
Clinton

*A civil rights demonstrator carries an American flag in Harlem, New York, in 1964.*

Hillary quickly got involved. She joined the campus Republican group. Most of the Wellesley students were Democrats, so Hillary didn't have much competition when she became president of the group. She also found herself changing from the way she'd been in Park Ridge. By the end of her freshman year, she no longer wore white blouses and pleated skirts. Now she wore long skirts and granny glasses. Her father disliked the changes in her appearance. He believed that people who wore less traditional clothing were liberal in their beliefs. He said he never would have let Hillary attend Wellesley if he'd known it would turn her into a Democrat!

Hillary also began getting involved in civil rights. As a freshman, she invited an African-American friend to attend an all-white church service with her. At the time, it was uncommon for blacks and whites to attend the same church. In her sophomore year, Hillary began to encourage Wellesley to admit more African-American students. She also said the college should hire more faculty members of color.

Her activism spread to other areas at her college. She campaigned to change curfew rules. She urged the school to end the rule that banned men from visiting Wellesley dormitories. She also asked the administration to use a pass-fail grading system. The natural-born leader couldn't help but lead. Usually, she was successful.

The other students quickly noticed the blue-eyed young woman who loved to talk politics and current events. They were drawn to her as a leader. In Hillary, they saw someone who could help them with their problems. She analyzed problems and formed solutions well. Then she motivated others to help her carry out those solutions.

Hillary's college days weren't all studying and activism, however. She dated boys and listened to music. She also loved to dance and exercise. Though she'd always followed the rules as a child, she began to relax a little during college. Wellesley had a ban on swimming in the lake on campus, called Lake Waban. Eventually, Hillary got brave enough to go swimming there anyway.

In April 1968, Martin Luther King, Jr., was assassinated. Some Wellesley students wanted to protest to show their anger about King's death. Hillary took charge and turned their feelings into something more productive. A month after the assassination, Hillary organized a teach-in in his honor. The teach-in featured special classes about King and his work.

*Wellesley College students, dressed in academic gowns, roll old-fashioned wooden hoops during the 105th Annual Hoop-Rolling Contest in April, 2000.*

By 1968, Hillary had become a Democrat. She campaigned for Eugene McCarthy to win the Democratic presidential nomination. She also campaigned for herself. One of her goals was to be president of student government. In her senior year, she achieved that goal. These experiences gave Hillary the opportunity to give many speeches. By the time she was in her early 20s, she already had professional public speaking skills.

Hillary's fellow students presented her with a special honor in the spring of 1969. Before that time, no Wellesley student had ever given the commencement speech at her own graduation ceremony. Hillary's classmates decided that she should be the first.

On graduation day, Hillary's speech followed the main speech by Edward Brooke, a senator from Massachusetts. Not surprisingly, Brooke's speech criticized students for protesting government actions, such as fighting in the Vietnam War. When Hillary reached the podium, she knew she had to address Brooke's criticisms. She put aside the speech she had prepared and spoke from her heart. She talked about the need to use politics for good.

"The challenge now," she said, "Is to practice politics as the art of making what appears to be impossible, possible." When she had made her point, she returned to her prepared speech. Hillary's honor as the first student to speak at a Wellesley commencement made her famous. She was featured in a 1969 issue of *Life* magazine.

By the time she graduated, Hillary had decided she wanted to attend law school. She was torn between attending law school at Harvard or Yale. During this time, she spoke with a Harvard law professor at a party. She told him she was debating between the two schools. "We don't need any more women," he said. That's all it took for Hillary to choose Yale.

*Hillary Rodham Clinton*

# An Advocate
# For Children

*T*he summer before starting law school, Hillary attended a conference sponsored by the League of Women Voters. Hillary was thrilled to be a part of the event. While there, she met many important people. After the conference, Hillary treated herself to a trip to Alaska. Alaska had become a state just 10 years earlier.

That fall, Hillary moved to New Haven, Connecticut. There, she started classes at Yale University Law School. She was one of only 30 women entering Yale Law School that fall. Yale was a demanding school, but Hillary maintained her usual good grades that first year.

That spring, Hillary heard Marian Wright Edelman speak at Yale. Edelman was the first African-American woman to become a lawyer in the state of Mississippi. She worked for an organization called the Children's Defense Fund. During her speech, Edelman talked about children and the law.

Edelman's speech sparked something in Hillary. Hillary had always been drawn to helping children. She remembered the heartbreaking scenes she had

*First Lady Hillary Rodham Clinton meets children at Mother Teresa's Sishu Vhavan Orphanage in Calcutta, India, in 1997.*

witnessed among the migrant children she met as a student. If she could make a difference, she wanted to use the law to help children.

After Edelman's speech, Hillary asked her for a job. Hillary spent that summer working with Edelman at the Children's Defense Fund. She worked to help children of migrant workers.

When Hillary returned to Yale, she volunteered in the Yale Child Studies Center. She also planned to stay at Yale an extra year to study the rights of children under the law. That fall, she met a handsome young man from Arkansas who was to change the course of her life.

# Meeting a Man From Arkansas

*H*illary Rodham knew who Bill Clinton was. She had heard him boasting about his home state of Arkansas. She knew he had come to Yale after spending two years at England's Oxford University as a Rhodes Scholar. What she didn't know was how much Bill Clinton knew about her.

Bill had been fascinated with Hillary for weeks. He'd heard her speak in a class they had together. He saw how people gravitated toward Hillary and how they loved talking with her. He quickly sensed her intelligence and confidence. He'd already heard she was the Wellesley graduate who made history with her commencement address.

Hillary recalled how they met. "Finally, one day he was standing outside the law school library. And I was in, trying to study, but I was kind of keeping my eye on him. And he kept kind of looking at me, and finally, I went up to him, and I said, 'You know, if we're going to keep looking at each other, we ought to at least know each other's name.'"

*Hillary Rodham Clinton and
President Bill Clinton in 1993.*

From that point on, Hillary and Bill became a team. Bill loved being with such an intelligent woman. Hillary enjoyed being with a man who wasn't afraid of her abilities. Bill made it clear that he planned to return to Arkansas and become governor. Hillary made it clear that she wanted to use her education to work for social change.

In the fall of 1970, Hillary began looking for a summer internship with a law firm that worked for social change. She found one in Oakland, California. The firm was defending members of the Black

*Two Black Panther members pose outside a meeting room.*

Panther Party. The Panthers were an African-American political organization. They encouraged African-Americans to defend themselves. They sought to restructure American society so that they could have more rights. Unlike Martin Luther King, Jr., the Panthers believed it was acceptable to use violence to achieve change. Their acts often got them into trouble with the law. During her internship, Hillary helped the firm defend some of the Panthers' members.

In the summer of 1972, Hillary moved to San Antonio, Texas, to work on Senator George McGovern's presidential campaign. She helped register Hispanic people to vote. Bill also moved to Texas to work on the McGovern campaign. The two spent the fall in Texas as well. Even though they had not attended their classes at Yale, they returned in time to take the fall final exams. They both passed their exams and graduated from Yale Law School in 1973.

Bill immediately returned to Arkansas to teach law at the University of Arkansas at Fayetteville. Hillary accepted a job with the Children's Defense Fund. She would be working with her friend Marian Wright Edelman. She spent six months working with Edelman before she received a call that pulled her into a historic event.

# Watergate

*I*n June 1972, five burglars were caught breaking into the Democratic National Committee headquarters. The headquarters was in the Watergate office and apartment complex in Washington, D.C. The burglars were there to bug the room. Listening in on important information could help Republican candidates win the election that fall.

The break-in investigation quickly unraveled a web of secrets. Investigators had reason to believe that many high-ranking government officials had known about and supported the break-in. Those officials included President Richard Nixon. Another scandal arose when investigators learned that officials had tried to cover up their involvement in the break-in.

In January 1974, the House Judiciary Committee was preparing to impeach President Nixon for his role in the Watergate scandal. They needed lawyers to help them make a case against Nixon. Rodham was among those that the committee asked to help. She gladly accepted the job, even though it meant working 18-hour days. Nixon resigned before the case went to trial. However, Rodham gained valuable experience and met important people.

*President Richard Nixon*

Now Rodham was at a career crossroads. She had her choice of jobs with famous law firms in New York City, Washington, D.C., and Chicago. Her friends knew she had a brilliant legal career ahead of her. Then she did something that shocked almost everyone. She decided to move to Arkansas.

Rodham had visited Arkansas the year before. She agreed with Clinton that it was a beautiful state. Yet what really brought her to the state was her heart. She told a close friend about Clinton, saying, "I love him."

# New Home In Arkansas

*H*illary Rodham got a job teaching law at the University of Arkansas at Fayetteville. It was the same school where Bill Clinton was teaching. She also set up a program to provide legal services for people at the university who could not afford them.

In 1974, Clinton ran for U.S. Congress. Rodham helped with his campaign, but he lost the race. During this time, Rodham thought a lot about her relationship with Clinton. She and Bill were opposites in many ways. He was charming and outgoing. She was cool and logical. He was the charismatic politician while she was the intellectual. But even though they had many differences, she felt a strong partnership with him.

In August 1975, Rodham took a trip back to Chicago and the East Coast to visit friends. Her friends encouraged her to leave Arkansas. They thought she'd been crazy to move there. She refused. "I didn't see anything out there that I thought was more exciting or challenging than what I had in front of me," she said of her trip.

*Arkansas governor Bill Clinton and Hillary Rodham at a White House dinner in 1979.*

When Rodham returned, Clinton picked her up at the airport. He drove her to a house they had seen before. She had commented to him that she liked the house. He told her he'd bought it! "I guess we'll have to get married now," he said. And on October 11, 1975, they did. Rodham chose to keep her maiden name. After the wedding, the newlyweds honeymooned in Mexico for two weeks along with Rodham's parents and two brothers.

The following year, Clinton decided to run for attorney general of Arkansas. Meanwhile, Rodham put her organizational skills to work on Jimmy Carter's presidential campaign. Carter won the election. Likewise, Clinton was elected attorney general of Arkansas.

The young couple moved to Little Rock, Arkansas, the state capital. Rodham took a job with the Rose Law Firm. At that time, Arkansas had few female lawyers. Many people refused to take her abilities as a lawyer seriously because she was a woman.

In 1978, Clinton ran for governor of Arkansas. He was elected and at the age of 32 became the nation's youngest governor. Rodham now was first lady of Arkansas. She also continued to work as an attorney. This bothered some people. They thought women should focus on taking care of their homes rather than having careers.

*President Jimmy Carter*

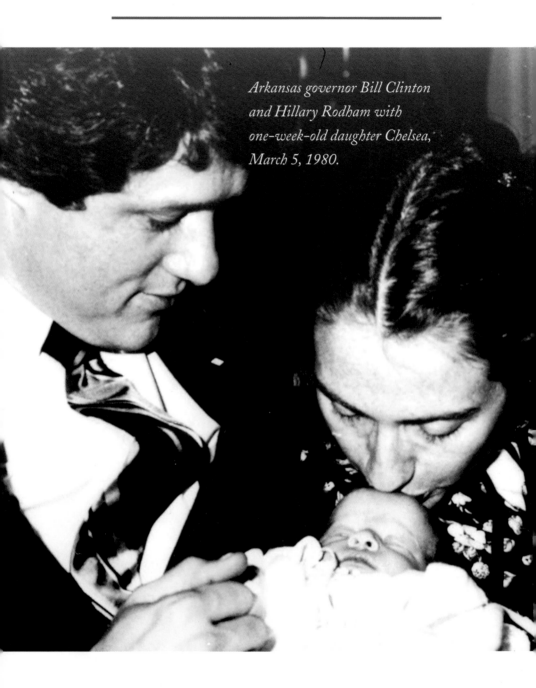

*Arkansas governor Bill Clinton and Hillary Rodham with one-week-old daughter Chelsea, March 5, 1980.*

People also criticized Rodham for keeping her maiden name after she married. And they criticized her for not paying more attention to her makeup, hair, and wardrobe.

Rodham was aware people were complaining about those things. She didn't let it bother her. She was busy. President Carter had appointed her to the board of a national organization that helped poor people get legal advice. She also helped start the Arkansas Advocates for Children and Families organization. Clinton appointed her to find ways to bring better medical care to people in rural Arkansas.

Rodham and Clinton also had a new project of their own. Their daughter, Chelsea Victoria Clinton, was born on February 27, 1980.

# Defeat and Depression

*G*overnor Clinton was up for re-election in 1980. This time, he lost. Rodham and Clinton agonized over the reasons. He may have lost because people couldn't accept that the first lady had kept her name or had her own career. Whatever the reason, her husband became depressed.

Despite Clinton's election loss, Rodham's career was in high gear. She was now a full partner at the Rose Law Firm. Twice the *National Law Journal* named her one of the 100 most influential lawyers in America. During this time, Clinton feared his political career was over. He took a job with a different law firm in Little Rock.

In the meantime, Rodham decided that if she had been part of the reason for her husband's defeat, she would change. She switched her name from Hillary Rodham to Hillary Rodham Clinton. She got contact lenses and began paying more attention to her hair, makeup, and clothes.

*Hillary Rodham Clinton in 1985.*

In 1982, Clinton ran for governor again. Rodham Clinton took her new look out on the campaign trail. The public noticed, and they seemed to appreciate it. Meanwhile, she showed the voters what a brilliant speaker and strategist she was on behalf of her husband, and he won the election.

For the next 10 years, Rodham Clinton was Arkansas's first lady. She also worked as a public servant. Governor Clinton appointed her to chair the Arkansas Education Standards Committee. Rodham Clinton oversaw her husband's plans to reform the state's education system. She visited every one of the state's 75 counties, talking with people about education. It was a long and painful process. Many people opposed some of the changes. Yet in the end, it was successful and the schools in Arkansas improved.

Rodham Clinton used her influence to help Arkansas children in other ways, too. She started a program to help low-income people prepare their children for school. She set up a special hospital nursery to care for critically ill infants.

*Arkansas governor Bill Clinton and Hillary Rodham Clinton celebrate his election victory.*

*Arkansas governor Bill Clinton and Hillary Rodham Clinton arrive for dinner at the White House, February 1986.*

In spite of her busy schedule, Rodham Clinton was a dedicated mother to Chelsea. She tried not to miss any of her daughter's games or performances. She helped Chelsea understand why some people said bad things about her father. She also taught Chelsea the importance of helping others.

By this time, people outside of Arkansas were taking notice of the Clintons. Some began talking about Governor Clinton running for president. In 1987, many people expected him to announce his candidacy. Instead, he said the time wasn't right. Chelsea was only seven, and he and his wife worried about the impact a campaign might have on her. People in Arkansas were also urging Rodham Clinton to run for Congress or take over as governor if her husband became president.

Rodham Clinton told them she wasn't interested in public office. Four years later, however, Governor Clinton said he was ready for a higher office. He announced he would run for president of the United States.

# On the Campaign Trail

*H*illary Rodham Clinton was familiar with campaigning. She had been running campaigns since she was in high school, and she was good at it. Her husband's presidential campaign put those skills to the ultimate test. There were seven people hoping to become the Democratic candidate.

The campaign spotlighted Rodham Clinton almost as much as her husband. Once again, she came under attack. Some people claimed clients of the Rose Law Firm had received special treatment because their lawyer, Rodham Clinton, was married to the governor. Others criticized her for keeping her maiden name as long as she had. Still others thought she went too far when she said children should have the right to sue their parents if they were treated poorly.

In March 1992, Rodham Clinton spoke with reporters to address criticisms of her career raised by another candidate. "I suppose I could have stayed home and baked cookies and had teas," she said. "But what I decided to do was fulfill my profession, which I entered before my husband was in public life." She

*President-elect Bill Clinton reaches into a crowd of supporters as his wife Hillary, and Tipper Gore cheer at the Old State House in Little Rock, Arkansas, November 3, 1992.*

went on to say she believed it was important that women had choices. She felt women should be allowed to be homemakers or career women, depending on what they wanted. That part of her remark, however, was not widely quoted. As a result, it appeared that Rodham Clinton disapproved of women who chose not to work outside the home.

If Rodham Clinton was a problem in her husband's campaign, she also was an asset. When he was accused of a 12-year affair with another woman, Rodham Clinton stood by his side. Her support helped him regain some credibility with voters. She helped him with speeches and listened to his ideas. Her problem-solving skills helped him refine those ideas before he presented them publicly.

Their hard work was rewarded in November 1992 when Governor Clinton was elected president.

# A Champion For Health Care

*H*illary Rodham Clinton was never one to sit on the sidelines. As first lady, she was no different. Less than a week after President Clinton was inaugurated, he appointed his wife to head his Task Force on National Health Care Reform. She immediately went to work meeting with leaders to discuss health care issues. Rodham Clinton's understanding of complex health care issues impressed even those people who were unsure how they felt about President Clinton.

Rodham Clinton and her staff began traveling around the country talking to people about health care. They also listened and worked to come up with solutions. When they were finished, they drafted a plan that was more than one thousand pages long.

Next, they presented their plan to Congress. In September 1993, the first lady appeared before five congressional committees for three days. She had no notes or references. She spoke about the health care plan from memory. When she was done, some committee members gave her a standing ovation.

Congress debated the Health Care Reform Plan for a year. In the end, the plan was not put into action. Critics said it would change the U.S. health care system too much. They also said it would cost too much for small businesses.

Rodham Clinton had put many hours into the plan. She had not been paid for her work. Regardless of this, many people resented her power as first lady. They believed she stayed with President Clinton because she wanted the power and career perks that came with being so close to the president. After the health care plan was defeated, the first lady took a less active role in public policy issues.

*First Lady Hillary Rodham Clinton testifies before Congress during hearings on health care reform, on September 28, 1993.*

# String of Scandals

*I*n 1993, Hillary Rodham Clinton found herself involved in a scandal. It involved a failed real estate investment that she and her husband had made in 1978. They formed the Whitewater Development Corporation, which tried to develop some land in Arkansas for home building. Because few people wanted to buy the land, the Clintons lost money. Their partners in the business also bought a small savings and loan. Unfortunately, the savings and loan later filed for bankruptcy. The government had to help, which cost taxpayers a lot of money. Some people said the Clintons had received some of the money that was not meant for them. This was not legal. An independent prosecutor investigated the matter.

The Whitewater investigation continued for five more years and spread to other areas of the Clintons' lives. In January 1996, the first lady testified before a grand jury regarding Whitewater, as it came to be known. It was the first time a first lady had done that. Neither she nor her husband was convicted of doing anything wrong. However, several of their

*Hillary Rodham Clinton answers reporters' questions during a news conference.*

former business partners were convicted of financial misdeeds.

The scandal intensified in January 1998. The prosecutor working on the Whitewater investigation expanded it to cover another matter. It involved a White House intern named Monica Lewinsky. The investigation concluded that President Clinton had an affair with the intern. The prosecutor said Clinton had lied about it while under oath. Lying under oath is a crime called perjury.

Both scandals were difficult for the first lady. Fortunately for Rodham Clinton, her father had raised her to survive in a tough world. She put on a brave face before the cameras and supported her husband. She told reporters the scandal was another example of her husband's political enemies trying to hurt him.

# Senator Clinton

*T*hroughout her time as first lady, Hillary Rodham Clinton worked to improve opportunities for women and children. She traveled around the world and spoke about women's rights. In 1995, she traveled to China to speak at the United Nations Fourth World Conference on Women. In 1996, she wrote a book called *It Takes a Village and Other Lessons Children Teach Us*. The book discussed how everyone is responsible for the welfare of the world's children. The book quickly became a best-seller.

As President Clinton's second term in the White House drew to a close, the first lady had a decision to make. What next? She had always been drawn to public service. Many people had encouraged her to run for office. She decided now was the time to do that.

In January 2000, the Clintons bought a home in Chappaqua, New York. The first lady spent her time there as her husband finished his term. That February, she announced she was seeking a New York Senate seat. Senator Daniel Patrick Moynihan was retiring.

The first lady hit the campaign trail with enthusiasm. She traveled the state talking to people about their concerns. Her opponent was New York City mayor Rudolph Giuliani. Giuliani later dropped out of the race. U.S. Representative Rick Lazio replaced Giuliani. On November 7, 2000, Hillary Rodham Clinton won the race and was elected to the U.S. Senate.

Hillary Rodham Clinton's victory made her the first first lady to be elected to the U.S. Senate. With more years ahead of her in the Senate, it is likely that there are even more firsts yet to come.

*Hillary Rodham Clinton announcing her candidacy for the U.S. Senate, on February 6, 2000.*

# Timeline

October 26, 1947: Hillary Diane Rodham is born in Chicago, Illinois.

1950: The Rodhams move to Park Ridge, a suburb of Chicago.

1965: Rodham graduates from Maine South High School and enters Wellesley College.

1969: Rodham begins Yale Law School.

1975: Rodham marries Bill Clinton.

1977: Rodham joins Rose Law Firm.

1978: Bill Clinton is elected governor of Arkansas.

1980: Chelsea Clinton is born.

1992: Bill Clinton is elected president of the United States. Rodham Clinton becomes first lady.

1993: Rodham Clinton is appointed to head the Task Force on National Health Care Reform.

2000: Rodham Clinton is elected to the United States Senate.

# Web Sites

Would you like to learn more about Hillary Rodham Clinton? Please visit **www.abdopub.com** to find up-to-date Web site links about Hillary Rodham Clinton. These links are routinely monitored and updated to provide the most current information available.

*Hillary Rodham Clinton with husband President Bill Clinton and daughter Chelsea.*

# Glossary

### activist
A person who works for political change.

### affair
A romantic relationship between two people who are not married to each other.

### assassinate
To murder a very important person.

### attorney general
The chief law officer of a national or state government.

### charismatic
Appealing to large numbers of people.

### Democratic Party
A political party that believes in social change and strong government.

### impeach
To have a trial to determine if a person should be removed from office.

## inaugurate

To be sworn into a political office.

## intern

A student who gets advanced training by working in his or her field.

## Ivy League

A group of eight academic institutions: Brown, Columbia, Cornell, Dartmouth, Harvard, University of Pennsylvania, Princeton, and Yale. The word *ivy* refers to the plants that climb over many of the old buildings on these school campuses.

## Republican Party

A political party that is conservative and believes in small government.

## savings and loan

A business similar to a bank where people can invest their money.

## Vietnam War

A long, failed attempt by the United States to stop North Vietnam from taking over South Vietnam from 1955-1975.

# Index